A Beginner's Guide to AI Agents:

Build Your Own AI Assistant

Table of Contents

Part 1: AI Agents Demystified

Welcome to Part 1 of our journey into the fascinating world of AI agents! If you've ever been curious about how your favorite digital assistants seem to understand you, or wondered how websites seem to know exactly what you're looking for, you're in the right place. This section is all about demystifying the magic behind these intelligent systems, breaking down complex concepts into simple, relatable ideas.

Imagine walking into a room filled with intricate machinery. At first glance, it might seem overwhelming, a jumble of wires and gears. But as we take a closer look, we begin to understand how each part works together to create something amazing. That's exactly what we'll be doing in Part 1. We'll be taking apart the "machinery" of AI agents, exploring their core components, and understanding how they function in our everyday lives.

We'll start by answering the fundamental question: what exactly are AI agents? We'll define them in simple terms, using examples you can easily relate to, like voice assistants and recommendation systems. We'll explore how these agents perceive their environment, make decisions, and take actions, just like we do. You'll discover that AI agents aren't just abstract concepts; they're the brains behind many of the smart technologies we use daily.

But understanding what AI agents are is just the beginning. We'll also delve into why they're so important in our world. From automating mundane tasks to solving complex problems, AI agents are revolutionizing industries and shaping our future. We'll explore real-world applications in healthcare, education, entertainment, and more, showing you how these intelligent systems are making a tangible difference in our lives.

One of the most exciting aspects of AI agents is their ability to understand and generate human-like language. This is where Large Language Models (LLMs) come in. We'll introduce you to these powerful tools, explaining how they enable AI agents to communicate with us in a natural and intuitive way. You'll learn how to "talk" to LLMs effectively, using prompts to get the information you need.

As we explore the capabilities of AI agents, we'll also address the important topic of ethics. We'll discuss the potential for AI bias, the need for fairness, and the importance of building safe and trustworthy systems. Through real-world scenarios and case studies, you'll gain a deeper understanding of the ethical considerations that guide AI development.

Part 1 is designed to be your friendly introduction to the world of AI agents. We'll use clear, concise language, avoid technical jargon, and provide plenty of relatable examples to make learning fun and engaging. By the end of this section, you'll have a solid foundation in the core concepts of AI agents, setting you up for the hands-on building experience in Part 2. So, let's embark on this exciting journey of discovery, and unveil the magic behind the machines!

Chapter 1: Welcome to the World of AI Agents!

Introduction: Setting the Stage

Hey there, future AI creators! Welcome to the very first chapter of our exciting adventure. We're about to explore a world that might seem like magic at first, but it's actually built on clever ideas and smart programming. We're talking about **AI agents** – those digital helpers that are popping up everywhere, from your phone to your favorite websites.

Imagine you have a super-smart assistant who can understand what you're saying, help you find information, and even perform tasks for you. That's essentially what an AI agent is. It's a computer program designed to act intelligently, just like a real person would. But instead of living in the real world, it lives inside computers and digital devices.

Now, you might be thinking, *'AI? That sounds complicated!'* But don't worry, we're going to break it all down into simple, easy-to-understand pieces. We'll start by understanding what AI agents are, why they're important, and where you can find them in your everyday life.

This chapter is all about getting you excited and comfortable with the idea of AI agents. We'll use lots of real-life examples and avoid confusing technical terms. By the end of this chapter, you'll have a clear understanding of what AI agents are and why they're becoming so important. So, let's get started on our journey into the world of AI agents!

What Are AI Agents?

So, what exactly is an AI agent? Let's start with a simple definition: **An AI agent is a computer program that can perceive its environment, make decisions, and take actions to achieve specific goals.**

Think of it like this: Imagine a little robot vacuum cleaner. It has sensors that allow it to 'see' the room, it has a brain that decides where to go, and it has wheels and brushes that allow it to 'act' by cleaning the floor. That's a very basic AI agent!

Here are some key characteristics of AI agents:

1. **Perception**: AI agents can 'see' or 'sense' their environment. This could be through cameras, microphones, sensors, or by reading data from a computer.

   - *Example*: Your phone's voice assistant 'hears' your voice through the microphone, and a website's recommendation system 'sees' what products you've viewed.

2. **Decision-Making**: AI agents can use rules or learning to make decisions about what to do next.

   - *Example*: A navigation app decides the best route to take based on traffic and road conditions. A chatbot decides what to say based on your questions.

3. **Action**: AI agents can 'act' on their decisions. This could be by moving, speaking, displaying information, or performing tasks on a computer.

   - *Example*: A self-driving car turns the steering wheel, a digital assistant plays music, and a smart thermostat adjusts the temperature.

4. **Goals**: AI agents are designed to achieve specific goals. This could be anything from cleaning a room to answering a question.

   - *Example*: A chess-playing AI agent's goal is to win the game, and a customer service chatbot's goal is to help you solve your problem.

Let's look at some relatable examples:

- **Siri or Google Assistant**: These are voice assistants that 'hear' your voice, 'understand' your requests, and 'act' by providing information, setting reminders, or playing music.

- **Recommendation Systems**: When you watch videos on YouTube or shop on Amazon, you see recommendations for other things you might like. These systems 'see' what you've watched or bought and 'decide' what else to show you.

- **Chatbots**: Many websites have chatbots that can answer your questions or help you find information. These bots 'read' your messages and 'decide' what to say in response.

- **Video Game AI**: In video games, the computer-controlled characters (NPCs) are AI agents. They 'see' what you're doing and 'decide' how to react.

These examples show that AI agents are already a big part of our lives. They're making things easier and more convenient, and they're becoming more and more intelligent all the time.

Why Are AI Agents Important?

Now that we know what AI agents are, let's talk about why they're so important. The truth is, AI agents are changing the world in many ways. Here are some of the reasons why:

1. **Automation**: AI agents can automate tasks that are repetitive, time-consuming, or dangerous for humans.

    - *Example*: In factories, robots (which are a type of AI agent) can assemble products faster and more accurately than humans. In customer service, chatbots can answer common questions, freeing up human agents to handle more complex issues.

2. **Efficiency**: AI agents can perform tasks faster and more efficiently than humans.

    - *Example*: Search engines use AI agents to index and rank websites, allowing us to find information in seconds. Navigation apps use AI agents to calculate the fastest route, saving us time and fuel.

3. **Personalization**: AI agents can personalize experiences to meet individual needs.

   - *Example*: Streaming services use AI agents to recommend movies and TV shows that you'll like. Social media platforms use AI agents to show you content that's relevant to your interests.

4. **Problem-Solving**: AI agents can help us solve complex problems that are difficult for humans to solve.

   - *Example*: In healthcare, AI agents can analyze medical images to detect diseases. In finance, AI agents can detect fraud and manage risk.

5. **Accessibility**: AI agents can make technology more accessible to people with disabilities.

   - *Example*: Voice assistants can help people with visual impairments use their phones. AI-powered translation tools can help people who speak different languages communicate.

Let's look at some real-world examples:

- **Healthcare**: AI agents are being used to develop new drugs, diagnose diseases, and personalize treatment plans.

- **Education**: AI agents are being used to create personalized learning experiences, provide feedback to students, and automate grading.

- **Transportation**: AI agents are being used to develop self-driving cars, optimize traffic flow, and improve public transportation.

- **Entertainment**: AI agents are being used to create video games, generate music, and write stories.

- **Business**: AI agents are being used to automate customer service, manage inventory, and analyze data.

These examples show that AI agents are having a significant impact on many different industries. They're making things more efficient, personalized, and accessible. As AI technology continues to advance, we can expect to see even more innovative applications of AI agents in the future.

But it's not just about big companies and fancy technology. AI agents can also be useful in your everyday life. Imagine having an AI agent that can help you:

- **Organize your schedule**: Remind you of appointments, deadlines, and tasks.

- **Find information**: Search the internet for answers to your questions.

- **Learn new things**: Provide you with personalized study materials and quizzes.

- **Be creative**: Help you brainstorm ideas, write stories, or generate art.

These are just a few examples of how AI agents can make your life easier and more productive. As you learn more about AI agents, you'll discover even more ways to use them in your daily life.

AI Agents in Everyday Life

You might not realize it, but AI agents are already a big part of your everyday life. Let's explore some examples that students can relate to:

1. **Homework Helpers**: Imagine an AI agent that can help you with your homework. You could ask it questions about math problems, science concepts, or history facts, and it would provide you with clear and helpful answers. It could even generate practice quizzes to help you study for tests.

   - *Example*: You could ask, *'What is the Pythagorean theorem?'* and the AI agent would provide a clear explanation and examples.

2. **Study Buddies**: An AI agent could act as your study buddy, helping you stay organized and motivated. It could create study schedules, remind you of deadlines, and even test you on the material you're learning.

   - *Example*: You could ask, *'Create a study schedule for my history test,'* and the AI agent would generate a personalized schedule with specific topics and time slots.

3. **Creative Tools**: AI agents can also be used to help you be creative. Imagine an AI agent that can help you write stories, poems, or even songs. You could give it a prompt or an idea, and it would generate creative content for you.

   - *Example*: You could ask, *'Write a short story about a robot that learns to love,'* and the AI agent would generate a creative story based on your prompt.

4. **Task Management Assistants**: An AI agent could help you manage your to-do list, set reminders, and keep track of your tasks. It could even prioritize your tasks based on deadlines or importance.

   - *Example*: You could say, *'Remind me to finish my science project by Friday,'* and the AI agent would set a reminder and check in with you as the deadline approaches.

These examples show how AI agents can make your life easier, more organized, and even more fun. As you continue reading this book, you'll learn how to build your own AI agents to do all these things and more!

Chapter 2: How AI Agents Think (The Basics)

Introduction: Setting the Stage

Alright, everyone! In Chapter 1, we got acquainted with AI agents and saw how they're popping up all around us. Now, let's peek under the hood and see how these agents actually think. Don't worry, we're not going to dive into super-complicated math or coding just yet. We're going to break down the thinking process of an AI agent into simple, easy-to-understand concepts.

Imagine you're teaching a puppy a new trick. You show it what to do (sensing), you give it a command (thinking), and then it performs the trick (acting). AI agents work in a similar way. They have ways of 'seeing' the world, they have 'brains' that make decisions, and they have ways of 'doing' things.

We'll start by exploring the three core components of how an AI agent works: **sensing, thinking, and acting**. We'll use simple analogies and real-world examples to make these concepts crystal clear. Then, we'll talk about how AI agents make decisions, using rules and learning. We'll even use some fun examples, like a robot vacuum cleaner deciding where to clean or a chatbot choosing a response, to make it even more relatable.

This chapter is all about building a solid foundation. We'll use visual aids like diagrams and flowcharts to help you visualize the concepts. By the end of this chapter, you'll have a clear understanding of how AI agents think, and you'll be one step closer to building your own!

Sensing, Thinking, Acting: The Core Components

Let's break down the thinking process of an AI agent into three key components: **sensing, thinking, and acting**.

1. **Sensing**:

   - Just like we use our eyes, ears, and other senses to perceive the world around us, AI agents use sensors to gather information about their environment.

   - These sensors can be anything from cameras and microphones to data inputs from a computer.

   - *Example*:

     - A self-driving car uses cameras and sensors to 'see' the road, traffic lights, and other vehicles.

     - A voice assistant like Siri uses a microphone to 'hear' your voice.

     - A website's recommendation system 'sees' what products you've viewed and what other users with similar interests have purchased.

   - The data gathered through sensing is then processed and interpreted by the AI agent's 'brain'.

2. **Thinking**:

   - This is where the AI agent makes decisions based on the information it has gathered.

- The 'thinking' process can involve using rules, algorithms, or even machine learning to determine the best course of action.

- *Example*:

  - A chess-playing AI agent 'thinks' about the best move to make based on the current board position and the opponent's moves.

  - A navigation app 'thinks' about the fastest route based on traffic conditions and road closures.

  - A chatbot 'thinks' about the correct response by searching for key words in your query.

- This is the part of the AI agent that most closely resembles human intelligence.

3. **Acting**:

  - Once the AI agent has made a decision, it needs to take action.

  - This could involve moving, speaking, displaying information, or performing tasks on a computer.

  - *Example*:

    - A robot arm in a factory 'acts' by assembling a product.

    - A digital assistant 'acts' by playing music or setting a reminder.

    - A smart thermostat 'acts' by adjusting the temperature.

- The action taken by the AI agent is determined by its 'thinking' process.

Let's use a simple analogy to illustrate these components: Imagine a robot vacuum cleaner.

- **Sensing**: The robot vacuum uses sensors to detect dirt and obstacles in the room.

- **Thinking**: The robot vacuum's 'brain' decides where to go next based on the information from its sensors.

- **Acting**: The robot vacuum moves around the room and uses its brushes to clean up the dirt.

This simple example shows how AI agents use sensing, thinking, and acting to achieve their goals.

Decision-Making Made Simple: How AI Agents Use Rules and Learning

Now, let's talk about how AI agents make decisions. There are two main ways: **using rules** and **using learning**.

1. **Rules**:

   - Some AI agents make decisions based on a set of predefined rules.

   - These rules are like 'if-then' statements that tell the AI agent what to do in different situations.

   - *Example*:

     - A simple chatbot might use rules like:

       - 'If the user says "hello", then respond with "Hi there!"'.

- 'If the user asks "what is the weather", then retrieve weather data and display it'.
  - A traffic light system uses rules like:
    - 'If the sensor detects a car, then change the light to green'.
- Rule-based AI agents are good for tasks that are predictable and well-defined.

2. **Learning**:

- Other AI agents use machine learning to make decisions.
- This involves training the AI agent on a large dataset, allowing it to learn patterns and relationships.
- *Example*:
  - A recommendation system learns your preferences by analyzing your past viewing or purchasing history.
  - A spam filter learns to identify spam emails by analyzing a large dataset of spam and non-spam emails.
  - A self-driving car learns to navigate roads by training on a massive amount of data from real-world driving scenarios.
- Machine learning allows AI agents to adapt to new situations and improve their performance over time.

Let's use some more fun examples:

- **Robot Vacuum Cleaner**:

- A simple robot vacuum might use rules like:

    - 'If the sensor detects dirt, then clean the area'.

    - 'If the sensor detects an obstacle, then change direction'.

- A more advanced robot vacuum might use machine learning to learn the layout of your house and optimize its cleaning path.

- **Chatbot Choosing a Response**:

    - A simple chatbot might use rules like:

        - 'If the user says "I want to buy a shoe", then send them to the shoes section of the website'.

    - A more advanced chatbot might use machine learning to understand the user's intent and provide more personalized responses.

- **Video Game AI**:

    - A simple video game AI might use rules like:

        - 'If the player is within range, then attack'.

    - A more advanced video game AI might use machine learning to learn the player's strategies and adapt its behavior.

These examples show that AI agents can use both rules and learning to make decisions. The choice of which method to use depends on the complexity of the task and the availability of data.

Visual Aids: Diagrams and Flowcharts

To help you visualize these concepts, let's use some diagrams and flowcharts.

1. **Sensing, Thinking, Acting Diagram**:

   - Imagine a simple diagram with three boxes: 'Sensing', 'Thinking', and 'Acting'.

   - Arrows connect the boxes, showing the flow of information.

   - This diagram helps to illustrate the sequential nature of the AI agent's thinking process.

2. **Decision-Making Flowchart**:

   - Imagine a flowchart showing the decision-making process of a robot vacuum cleaner.

   - The flowchart might start with a question like 'Is there dirt?'.

   - If the answer is 'yes', the flowchart might lead to an action like 'Clean the area'.

   - If the answer is 'no', the flowchart might lead to an action like 'Move to next area'.

   - This flowchart helps to visualize how the robot vacuum uses rules to make decisions.

These visual aids can make it easier to understand how AI agents think and make decisions.

Fun Examples: A Robot Vacuum Deciding Where to Clean or a Chatbot Choosing a Response

Let's bring these concepts to life with some fun examples.

1. **Robot Vacuum Deciding Where to Clean**:

   - Imagine a robot vacuum that uses machine learning to learn the layout of your house.

- It starts by randomly exploring the house and cleaning up dirt.

- Over time, it learns which areas are more likely to be dirty and which areas are less likely to be dirty.

- It also learns how to navigate around obstacles and avoid getting stuck.

- Eventually, it develops an optimal cleaning path that covers the entire house efficiently.

2. **Chatbot Choosing a Response**:

- Imagine a chatbot that uses machine learning to understand the user's intent.

- When you ask a question, the chatbot analyzes the words and context to determine what you're looking for.

- For example, if you ask, *'What's the best way to study for a test?'*, the chatbot might respond with tips like *'Create a study schedule and take regular breaks.'*

- Over time, the chatbot learns from user interactions and improves its responses.

These examples show how AI agents use sensing, thinking, and acting to perform tasks and make decisions. By understanding these core components, you're well on your way to building your own AI agents!

Chapter 3: Meet the LLMs: Your AI Agent's Brain

Introduction: Setting the Stage

Welcome to a chapter that's going to unlock a whole new level of understanding about AI agents! We've talked about how agents

sense, think, and act, and how they use rules and learning. But what if we want our agents to understand and generate human-like language? That's where Large Language Models, or LLMs, come into play.

Think of LLMs as the super-smart brains that allow AI agents to understand and use language in a way that feels natural and intuitive. They're like the magic behind chatbots that can hold conversations, writing assistants that can help you compose emails, and even creative tools that can generate stories and poems.

In this chapter, we're going to demystify these powerful tools. We'll start by explaining what LLMs are and how they work, using simple analogies and relatable examples. Then, we'll explore how LLMs help AI agents understand and generate human-like language. We'll also dive into the art of prompt engineering, which is like learning how to 'talk' to LLMs effectively.

This chapter is all about empowering you to harness the power of LLMs. We'll use fun examples, like creating a joke-telling AI or a story generator, to make learning engaging and enjoyable. By the end of this chapter, you'll have a solid understanding of how LLMs work and how you can use them to build intelligent AI agents.

What Are Large Language Models

Let's start with the basics: What exactly are Large Language Models? Simply put, LLMs are a type of artificial intelligence that can understand and generate human-like language. They're called 'large' because they're trained on massive amounts of text data, which allows them to learn the patterns and relationships between words and phrases.

Think of it like this: Imagine you're learning a new language. You start by memorizing vocabulary and grammar rules. But to truly master the language, you need to immerse yourself in it, reading books, watching movies, and having conversations with native speakers. LLMs work in a similar way. They're trained on vast amounts of text data from the internet, which allows them to learn the nuances of language, from grammar and vocabulary to style and tone.

Here are some key characteristics of LLMs:

- **Training Data:** LLMs are trained on massive datasets of text and code. This data can include books, articles, websites, and even code repositories.
- **Neural Networks:** LLMs use neural networks, which are complex mathematical models that can learn from data. These networks are designed to recognize patterns and relationships in the training data.
- **Transformer Architecture:** Many modern LLMs are based on the transformer architecture, which is particularly effective at processing sequential data like text.
- **Language Generation:** LLMs can generate text that is coherent, grammatically correct, and often indistinguishable from human-written text.
- **Contextual Understanding:** LLMs can understand the context of a conversation or a piece of text, allowing them to provide more relevant and accurate responses.

Let's use some relatable examples to illustrate how LLMs work:

- **ChatGPT:** This is a popular chatbot that uses an LLM to generate human-like responses to your questions and prompts. It can write essays, summarize articles, and even generate code.
- **Google Bard:** Similar to ChatGPT, Google Bard uses an LLM to provide information, answer questions, and generate creative content.
- **Writing Assistants:** Many writing tools use LLMs to help you improve your writing. They can check your grammar and

spelling, suggest alternative phrasing, and even help you generate ideas.

These examples show that LLMs are powerful tools that can be used to create a wide range of applications. They're making it easier for us to communicate with computers and for computers to communicate with us.

How LLMs Help AI Agents: Understanding and Generating Human-Like Language

Now, let's explore how LLMs help AI agents understand and generate human-like language.

- **Natural Language Understanding (NLU):**
  - LLMs enable AI agents to understand the meaning behind human language.
  - This involves tasks like:
    - **Sentiment Analysis:** Determining the emotional tone of a piece of text.
    - **Named Entity Recognition:** Identifying people, places, and things in a text.
    - **Question Answering:** Understanding a question and providing a relevant answer.
  - *Example:*
    - You ask a chatbot, "I'm feeling really stressed today." The LLM can perform sentiment analysis to understand that you're feeling negative. It can then provide you with helpful resources or suggestions for relaxation.
- **Natural Language Generation (NLG):**
  - LLMs enable AI agents to generate text that is human-like and coherent.
  - This involves tasks like:

- **Text Summarization:** Condensing a long article into a shorter summary.
- **Creative Writing:** Generating stories, poems, and scripts.
- **Dialogue Generation:** Creating natural-sounding conversations.
  - *Example:*
    - You ask a chatbot to write a short poem about nature. The LLM can generate a poem that is both creative and grammatically correct.
- **Contextual Awareness:**
  - LLMs can maintain context throughout a conversation, allowing AI agents to provide more relevant and personalized responses.
  - *Example:*
    - You ask a chatbot, "What's the weather like today?" The chatbot provides the current weather forecast. Then, you ask, "And what about tomorrow?" The chatbot remembers the context of the previous question and provides the forecast for tomorrow.

LLMs are making AI agents more versatile and user-friendly. They're enabling us to create AI agents that can:

- **Hold natural conversations:** Chatbots that can engage in meaningful dialogue.
- **Provide personalized assistance:** Virtual assistants that can understand your needs and preferences.
- **Generate creative content:** Writing tools that can help you brainstorm ideas and create content.

These capabilities are opening up new possibilities for AI agents in various fields, from customer service and education to entertainment and research.

Prompt Engineering Explained Simply

Now, let's talk about prompt engineering. This is the art of crafting effective prompts that guide LLMs to generate the desired output. Think of a prompt as a set of instructions or a question that you give to an LLM.

Here are some key principles of prompt engineering:

- **Be Clear and Specific:** The more specific your prompt, the better the LLM will be able to understand your request.
  - *Example:* Instead of saying, "Write a story," say, "Write a short story about a robot that learns to love."
- **Provide Context:** Give the LLM enough context to understand your request.
  - *Example:* If you want the LLM to summarize an article, provide the article or a link to it.
- **Use Examples:** If you want the LLM to generate a specific type of output, provide examples of what you're looking for.
  - *Example:* If you want the LLM to write a poem in a specific style, provide an example of a poem in that style.
- **Iterate and Refine:** Don't be afraid to experiment with different prompts and refine them until you get the desired output.

Let's look at some examples:

- **Good Prompt:** "Write a short paragraph summarizing the main points of this article: [link to article]."
- **Bad Prompt:** "Summarize this."
- **Good Prompt:** "Write a joke about a cat."
- **Bad Prompt:** "Tell me something funny."

Prompt engineering is an iterative process. You may need to try several different prompts before you get the desired output. But with practice, you'll become more proficient at crafting effective prompts.

By mastering prompt engineering, you can unlock the full potential of LLMs and create AI agents that are truly intelligent and helpful.

Chapter 4: AI Agents and Ethics: Being Responsible

Introduction: Setting the Stage

Artificial Intelligence (AI) is no longer a futuristic concept—it's here, and it's transforming our world. From virtual assistants like Siri and Alexa to advanced systems that diagnose diseases or drive cars, AI agents are becoming an integral part of our daily lives. But with great power comes great responsibility. As AI systems grow more sophisticated, so do the ethical challenges they present. How do we ensure that these powerful tools are used for good? How do we prevent them from causing harm, perpetuating bias, or undermining privacy? These are the questions we'll explore in this chapter.

Why Ethics Matters in AI

Ethics is the study of what is right and wrong, and in the context of AI, it's about ensuring that these systems are designed and used in ways that benefit humanity. AI agents, powered by Large Language Models (LLMs) and other advanced technologies, have the potential to revolutionize industries, solve complex problems, and improve lives. However, they can also perpetuate inequality, invade privacy, and even cause harm if not developed responsibly.

Consider this: AI systems are only as good as the data they're trained on and the intentions of their creators. If the data is biased, the AI will be biased. If the creators prioritize profit over people, the AI may end up harming users. That's why ethics isn't just an afterthought—it's a core part of building trustworthy AI systems.

The Societal Impact of AI

AI is not just a technical tool; it's a societal force. It influences how we work, communicate, and make decisions. For example:

- **Economic Impact**: AI is automating jobs, creating new industries, and reshaping the global economy. While this can lead to increased efficiency, it also raises concerns about job displacement and economic inequality.

- **Social Impact**: AI systems shape our online experiences, from the news we see to the ads we're shown. This can influence public opinion, reinforce stereotypes, and even manipulate behavior.

- **Cultural Impact**: AI is changing how we create and consume art, music, and literature. While this opens up new possibilities, it also raises questions about authorship, creativity, and intellectual property.

Given this far-reaching impact, it's crucial that we approach AI development with a strong ethical foundation. This chapter will guide you through the key ethical principles, challenges, and strategies for building responsible AI systems.

Why Ethics Matters in AI: Simple Scenarios

To understand why ethics is so important in AI, let's explore some simple scenarios that illustrate the ethical dilemmas AI systems can create.

Scenario 1: Biased Recommendations

Imagine an AI agent that recommends job applicants to a company. This agent is trained on data from past hires, which mostly includes men. As a result, the agent starts recommending mostly male applicants, even if equally qualified women apply.

Ethical Dilemma: This is an example of bias. The AI agent is making unfair decisions based on past data, which can perpetuate discrimination.

Discussion: Bias in AI systems often stems from biased training data. If historical hiring practices favored men, the AI will learn to do the same. This not only harms qualified women but also reinforces systemic inequality.

Potential Solutions:

- Use diverse training data that represents a wide range of people and perspectives.

- Implement fairness algorithms to adjust the AI's decision-making process.

- Regularly audit the AI system for bias and take corrective action.

Scenario 2: Privacy Concerns

Imagine an AI agent that collects data about your online activity. This data is used to personalize your experience, but it could also be used to track your movements, predict your behavior, or even sell your personal information.

Ethical Dilemma: This raises concerns about privacy. How much data should AI agents collect? Who owns that data? How is it used?

Discussion: Privacy is a fundamental human right, but AI systems often rely on vast amounts of personal data to function effectively. Striking a balance between utility and privacy is a major ethical challenge.

Potential Solutions:

- Implement data minimization practices, collecting only the data necessary for the task.

- Use encryption and anonymization techniques to protect user data.

- Be transparent about data collection practices and give users control over their data.

Scenario 3: Autonomous Weapons

Imagine AI agents that are used in weapons systems. These agents can make decisions about who to target without human intervention.

Ethical Dilemma: This raises serious questions about accountability. Who is responsible if an AI weapon makes a mistake? Should AI agents be allowed to make life-or-death decisions?

Discussion: Autonomous weapons represent one of the most controversial applications of AI. Delegating life-or-death decisions to machines raises profound moral and legal questions.

Potential Solutions:

- Advocate for international bans on autonomous weapons.

- Ensure human oversight in all critical decision-making processes.

- Develop ethical guidelines for the use of AI in military applications.

Scenario 4: Job Displacement

Imagine AI agents that automate many jobs. This could lead to widespread unemployment and economic inequality.

Ethical Dilemma: How do we prepare for a future where AI agents take over many jobs? How do we ensure everyone benefits from AI technology?

Discussion: While AI can increase productivity and create new opportunities, it also poses a threat to traditional jobs. Addressing this challenge requires proactive measures.

Potential Solutions:

- Invest in education and retraining programs to help workers transition to new roles.

- Implement policies like universal basic income to support those affected by job displacement.

- Encourage the development of AI systems that augment human capabilities rather than replace them.

Scenario 5: Misinformation and Deepfakes

Imagine an AI agent that generates realistic but fake news articles or videos. These deepfakes could be used to spread misinformation, manipulate public opinion, or damage reputations.

Ethical Dilemma: How do we prevent AI from being used to deceive or harm others? How do we balance freedom of expression with the need to combat misinformation?

Discussion: Deepfakes and AI-generated content are becoming increasingly sophisticated, making it harder to distinguish between real and fake information. This poses a significant threat to trust and democracy.

Potential Solutions:

- Develop tools to detect and flag deepfakes and misinformation.

- Promote media literacy to help people critically evaluate information.

- Establish regulations to hold creators of harmful deepfakes accountable.

Avoiding Bias and Being Fair

One of the biggest ethical challenges in AI is avoiding bias. Bias occurs when an AI agent makes unfair or discriminatory decisions based on its training data. Let's explore how we can address this issue.

Understanding Bias in AI

Bias in AI systems can take many forms:

- **Data Bias**: The training data is unrepresentative or reflects historical prejudices.

- **Algorithmic Bias**: The algorithm itself introduces bias, even if the data is fair.

- **Interaction Bias**: Users interact with the system in ways that reinforce bias.

Strategies for Avoiding Bias

1. **Use Diverse Training Data**: Ensure that the data used to train AI systems represents a wide range of people and perspectives.

2. **Monitor for Bias**: Regularly audit AI systems for biased outcomes and take corrective action.

3. **Implement Fairness Algorithms**: Use techniques like adversarial debiasing or reweighting to mitigate bias.

4. **Involve Diverse Teams**: Include people from diverse backgrounds in the design and development of AI systems to identify and address potential biases.

Case Study: AI in Hiring

Consider an AI system designed to screen job applicants. If the training data primarily consists of resumes from men, the system may unfairly favor male candidates. To address this:

- Gather resumes from a diverse pool of applicants.

- Use fairness algorithms to adjust the system's decision-making process.

- Consult with experts in diversity and inclusion to ensure the system is fair.

Keeping AI Agents Safe and Helpful

Building trustworthy AI systems also means keeping them safe and helpful. Here are some strategies to achieve this.

1. Test Thoroughly

Before deploying an AI system, test it extensively to identify potential issues. This includes:

- **Unit Testing**: Testing individual components of the system.

- **Integration Testing**: Ensuring that all components work together seamlessly.

- **Stress Testing**: Evaluating the system's performance under extreme conditions.

2. Implement Safety Measures

Build safeguards into AI systems to prevent harm. For example:

- A self-driving car could be programmed to avoid exceeding speed limits.

- A healthcare AI system could include checks to prevent incorrect diagnoses.

3. Provide Clear Instructions

Give AI systems clear and specific instructions to prevent unintended behavior. For example:

- A chatbot could be programmed to avoid offensive language.

- A recommendation system could be designed to prioritize user preferences.

4. Monitor and Update

Continuously monitor AI systems after deployment and update them as needed. This includes:

- Addressing new ethical challenges.

- Improving performance based on user feedback.

5. Ensure Human Oversight

In many cases, it's important to keep humans in the loop. For example:

- A medical AI system could provide recommendations, but a doctor would make the final decision.

- A financial AI system could flag potential fraud, but a human analyst would investigate further.

Real-World Examples: Case Studies of Ethical AI in Action

Let's look at some real-world examples of ethical AI in action.

1. AI for Accessibility

AI-powered tools are helping people with disabilities. For example:

- Speech recognition systems enable people with hearing impairments to communicate.

- Computer vision systems assist people with visual impairments in navigating their environment.

2. AI for Environmental Protection

AI is being used to monitor and protect the environment. For example:

- AI-powered drones detect deforestation and track wildlife populations.

- Machine learning models predict climate change impacts and inform policy decisions.

3. AI for Healthcare

AI is revolutionizing healthcare. For example:

- AI-powered image analysis helps doctors detect diseases like cancer.

- Natural language processing systems analyze medical records to identify trends and improve patient care.

4. AI in Education

AI is personalizing learning and improving access to education. For example:

- Adaptive learning platforms tailor content to individual students' needs.

- AI-powered translation tools break down language barriers in classrooms.

Conclusion: Shaping the Future of AI Responsibly

As we conclude this chapter, it's clear that ethics is not just an afterthought in AI development—it's a fundamental part of creating systems that benefit society. By prioritizing fairness, transparency, accountability, privacy, and safety, we can ensure that AI serves as a force for good.

The journey toward responsible AI is ongoing, and it requires collaboration, vigilance, and a commitment to learning. Together, we can build a future where AI is not only powerful but also just, equitable, and beneficial for all.

Part 2: Building Your First AI Agents (Hands-On)

Chapter 5: Setting Up Your AI Agent Lab (Free Tools!)

Introduction: Setting the Stage

Welcome to the exciting part of your AI journey—building your very own AI Agent Lab! In this chapter, we'll roll up our sleeves and dive into the practical side of AI development. You'll learn how to set up a workspace where you can experiment, create, and bring your AI ideas to life. The best part? Everything we'll use is free and accessible to anyone with an internet connection.

Think of this chapter as your guide to building a personal AI playground. Just like a scientist needs a lab or an artist needs a studio, you need a workspace to create and experiment with AI agents. We'll use **Python**, a beginner-friendly programming language, and **Google Colab**, a free online platform that lets you write and run code without needing to install anything on your computer.

By the end of this chapter, you'll have a fully functional AI Agent Lab, equipped with all the tools you need to start building your own AI projects. Let's get started!

Introduction to Python

Before we dive into building AI agents, let's get familiar with Python, the programming language we'll be using. Python is like the Swiss Army knife of coding—it's versatile, easy to learn, and widely used in AI development. Even if you've never written a line of code before, don't worry! We'll start with the basics and build up from there.

Why Python?

Python is the go-to language for AI and machine learning because:

- It's **easy to read and write**, making it perfect for beginners.

- It has a **huge community** of developers, so there are plenty of resources and libraries to help you.

- It's **powerful** enough to handle complex AI tasks.

Basic Python Concepts

Let's start with some fundamental Python concepts that you'll use in your AI projects.

1. Variables

Variables are like containers that store information. For example:

python
Copy

```
name = "AI Agent"
age = 1
is_learning = True
```

Here, `name`, `age`, and `is_learning` are variables that hold different types of data.

2. Data Types

Python uses different data types to represent different kinds of information:

- **Strings**: Text enclosed in quotes (e.g., `"Hello, world!"`).

- **Integers**: Whole numbers (e.g., `10`).

- **Floats**: Decimal numbers (e.g., `3.14`).

- **Booleans**: True or false values (e.g., `True`).

3. Print Statements

To display information, we use the `print()` function:

python
Copy

```
print("Hello, world!")
print(name)
```

This will print the text `"Hello, world!"` and the value of the `name` variable.

4. If Statements

If statements allow us to make decisions based on conditions:

python
Copy

```
if age > 0:
    print("The AI agent is alive!")
```

This will only print the message if the `age` variable is greater than `0`.

5. Loops

Loops allow us to repeat a set of instructions multiple times:

python
Copy

```python
for i in range(5):
    print(i)
```

This will print the numbers 0 through 4.

6. Functions

Functions are reusable blocks of code that perform a specific task:

python
Copy

```python
def greet(name):
    print(f"Hello, {name}!")

greet("Alice")
```

This will print "Hello, Alice!".

Google Colab: Your Free AI Agent Workspace

Now that we've covered the basics of Python, let's set up your AI Agent Lab using **Google Colab**. Google Colab is a free, cloud-based platform that lets you write and run Python code in your web browser. It's perfect for beginners because you don't need to install anything on your computer.

1. Getting Started with Google Colab

1. **Open Google Colab**:

    - Go to colab.research.google.com.

    - If you're not already logged in to your Google account, you'll be prompted to do so.

2. **Create a New Notebook**:

- Click on the `New Notebook` button at the bottom right of the screen.

- A new notebook will open, which is essentially a blank canvas for writing and running Python code.

2. Understanding the Colab Interface

The Colab interface is divided into **cells**. There are two types of cells:

- **Code Cells**: These are where you write and run Python code.

- **Text Cells**: These are where you write text, add images, and format your notebook.

To create a new cell, hover your mouse between existing cells and click the `+ Code` or `+ Text` button that appears. To run a code cell, click the `play` button that appears when you hover over the cell, or press `Shift+Enter`.

3. Running Your First Code

Let's run some Python code in Colab to make sure everything is working:

python
Copy

```
print("Welcome to your AI Agent Lab!")
```

Click the `play` button to run the code. You should see the message `"Welcome to your AI Agent Lab!"` printed below the cell.

4. Installing Libraries

We'll be using various Python libraries to build our AI agents. These libraries provide pre-written code that we can use in our projects. To install a library, we use the `pip install` command. For example, to install the `requests` library, type the following code in a code cell and run it:

python
Copy

```
!pip install requests
```

The `!` symbol tells Colab to run the command in the terminal.

5. Using API Keys

Some AI services, like OpenAI, require API keys to access their services. An API key is like a password that grants you access to the service. To use an API key in Colab, you can store it as an environment variable:

python
Copy

```
import os
os.environ["OPENAI_API_KEY"] = "YOUR_API_KEY"
```

Replace `"YOUR_API_KEY"` with your actual API key. **Important**: Never share your API keys with anyone!

6. Connecting to Google Drive

You can connect your Colab notebook to your Google Drive to save and load files. To connect to Google Drive, use the following code:

python
Copy

```
from google.colab import drive
drive.mount('/content/drive')
```

This will prompt you to authorize Colab to access your Google Drive.

Installing Necessary Tools

With our Python environment up and running in Google Colab, we need to add a few more specialized tools to our AI Agent Lab. These tools are Python libraries that contain code written by other developers, specifically designed to help us build AI agents more efficiently.

1. LangChain

LangChain is a framework that makes it easier to work with Large Language Models (LLMs). It provides tools for creating chains of prompts, managing memory, and connecting to external data sources. To install LangChain, type the following code in a Colab cell and run it:

python
Copy

```
!pip install langchain
```

2. OpenAI

OpenAI provides powerful LLMs like GPT-3 and GPT-4. To use these models, you'll need to install the OpenAI library:

python
Copy

```
!pip install openai
```

3. Hugging Face Transformers

Hugging Face is a popular platform for working with pre-trained AI models. To install the Transformers library, use:

python
Copy

```
!pip install transformers
```

4. NumPy and Pandas

NumPy and Pandas are essential libraries for working with data:

python
Copy

```
!pip install numpy pandas
```

5. Matplotlib and Seaborn

These libraries are used for data visualization:

python
Copy

```
!pip install matplotlib seaborn
```

Building Your First AI Agent

Now that our lab is set up, let's build a simple AI agent—a chatbot! Here's how:

1. Import Libraries

First, import the necessary libraries:

python
Copy

```
import openai
import os
```

2. Set Up the OpenAI API Key

Set your OpenAI API key as an environment variable:

python
Copy

```
os.environ["OPENAI_API_KEY"] = "YOUR_API_KEY"
```

3. Create the Chatbot

Use the OpenAI API to create a chatbot:

python
Copy

```python
def chatbot(prompt):
    response = openai.Completion.create(
        engine="text-davinci-003",
        prompt=prompt,
        max_tokens=50
    )
    return response.choices[0].text.strip()

# Test the chatbot
print(chatbot("Hello, how are you?"))
```

Conclusion: Your AI Agent Lab is Ready!

Congratulations! You've set up your AI Agent Lab and built your first AI agent. With Python, Google Colab, and the tools we've installed, you're ready to start experimenting and creating your own AI projects. Remember, the key to mastering AI is practice and curiosity. Keep exploring, keep building, and most importantly, have fun!

Chapter 6: Your First Simple AI Agent (Rule-Based)

Introduction: Setting the Stage

Welcome to the hands-on part of your AI journey—building your very first AI agent! In this chapter, we'll create a simple, rule-based chatbot using Python and the Google Colab environment you set up in the previous chapter. If you're new to coding, don't worry! We'll take it step by step, ensuring everything is clear and easy to follow.

Rule-based AI agents are a fantastic starting point because they're straightforward and easy to understand. These agents operate based on a set of predefined "if-then" rules, which tell the agent how to respond to different inputs. Think of it like teaching a robot to follow a set of instructions.

We'll start by building a basic chatbot that can respond to simple greetings and questions. Then, we'll explore how to create more complex rules and add functionality to make the chatbot more engaging. Along the way, we'll use fun examples like a weather bot and a trivia bot to bring the concepts to life.

By the end of this chapter, you'll have a working chatbot that you can customize and share with your friends. Let's dive in and start building!

Building a Basic Chatbot

Let's start by building a basic chatbot that can respond to simple greetings and questions. This chatbot will follow a set of rules to determine how to respond to user input.

Step 1: Open Google Colab

1. Open your Google Colab notebook that you set up in the previous chapter.

2. Create a new code cell by clicking the + Code button.

Step 2: Write the Code

Type the following code into the code cell:

python
Copy

```
def chatbot():
    print("Hello! I'm your simple chatbot.")

    while True:
```

```
        user_input = input("You: ")

        if user_input.lower() == "hello" or
user_input.lower() == "hi":
            print("Chatbot: Hello there!")
        elif user_input.lower() == "how are you?":
            print("Chatbot: I'm doing well, thank
you!")
        elif user_input.lower() == "bye" or
user_input.lower() == "goodbye":
            print("Chatbot: Goodbye!")
            break
        else:
            print("Chatbot: I'm sorry, I don't
understand.")

chatbot()
```

Step 3: Run the Code

1. Click the `play` button to run the code.

2. You should see the message `"Hello! I'm your simple chatbot."` printed below the code cell.

3. Type a message in the input box and press `Enter`. The chatbot will respond based on the rules we defined in the code.

Explanation of the Code

- `def chatbot():`: This defines a function called `chatbot()`. Functions are blocks of code that perform specific tasks.

- `print("Hello! I'm your simple chatbot.")`: This prints a greeting message.

- `while True:`: This creates an infinite loop, meaning the chatbot will keep running until we tell it to stop.

- `user_input = input("You: ")`: This gets input from the user and stores it in the `user_input` variable.

- `if user_input.lower() == "hello" or user_input.lower() == "hi":`: This checks if the user's input is `"hello"` or `"hi"` (ignoring case). If it is, the chatbot responds with `"Hello there!"`.

- `elif:`: This is short for "else if" and allows us to check for multiple conditions.

- `break:`: This stops the loop, ending the chatbot.

- `else:`: If none of the `if` or `elif` conditions are met, the chatbot responds with `"I'm sorry, I don't understand."`

- `chatbot():`: This calls the `chatbot()` function, which starts the chatbot.

Creating Simple "If-Then" Rules

Now that we've built a basic chatbot, let's explore how to create more complex rules and add functionality to make it more engaging.

1. Add More Rules

We can add more `if-then` rules to our chatbot to make it respond to more questions. For example, let's add a rule to respond to the question `"what is your name?"`:

python
Copy

```
elif user_input.lower() == "what is your name?":
    print("Chatbot: My name is Chatbot.")
```

2. Use Variables

We can use variables to store information and use it in our rules. For example, let's store the user's name and use it in our responses:

python
Copy

```python
elif "my name is" in user_input.lower():
    name = user_input.split("my name is ")[1]
    print(f"Chatbot: Hello, {name}!")
```

3. Use Random Responses

To make our chatbot's responses more varied, we can use the random library:

python
Copy

```python
import random

responses = ["That's interesting!", "Tell me more!", "I see."]

elif user_input.lower() == "tell me a joke":
    print(random.choice(responses))
```

4. Fun Examples: Weather Bot

Let's create a simple weather bot that can tell us the weather:

python
Copy

```python
elif user_input.lower() == "what is the weather?":
    # In a real application, you would use an API to
get weather data.
    print("Chatbot: It's sunny today!")
```

5. Fun Examples: Trivia Bot

Let's create a simple trivia bot that can ask us questions:

python
Copy

```python
elif user_input.lower() == "play trivia":
    print("Chatbot: What is the capital of France?")
    answer = input("You: ")
```

```python
if answer.lower() == "paris":
    print("Chatbot: Correct!")
else:
    print("Chatbot: Incorrect!")
```

Making Your Agent Respond to User Input

Let's make our agent more interactive by allowing it to respond to user input in more dynamic ways.

1. Using String Manipulation

We can use string manipulation techniques to extract information from user input. For example, let's extract the user's name from a sentence like "My name is John":

python
Copy

```python
elif "my name is" in user_input.lower():
    name = user_input.split("my name is ")[1]
    print(f"Chatbot: Nice to meet you, {name}!")
```

2. Using Regular Expressions

Regular expressions are powerful tools for pattern matching. We can use them to extract specific information from user input:

python
Copy

```python
import re

elif re.search(r"\d+", user_input):
    numbers = re.findall(r"\d+", user_input)
    print(f"Chatbot: I found the numbers: {numbers}")
```

3. Interactive Coding Exercises

Let's create some interactive coding exercises to make our agent more engaging. For example, we can create a simple calculator:

python
Copy

```python
elif "calculate" in user_input.lower():
    try:
        expression = user_input.split("calculate ")[1]
        result = eval(expression)
        print(f"Chatbot: The result is: {result}")
    except:
        print("Chatbot: I'm sorry, I cannot calculate
that.")
```

4. Visual Aids

To make the examples clearer, include screenshots of the code and
the chatbot's responses. Use code snippets to highlight specific parts
of the code and explain their functionality.

Conclusion: Your First AI Agent is Ready!

Congratulations! You've built your first AI agent—a rule-based
chatbot. By creating simple "if-then" rules, you've taught your
chatbot how to respond to user input in a structured way. You've
also explored how to make your chatbot more interactive and
engaging by adding variables, random responses, and fun examples
like a weather bot and a trivia bot.

This is just the beginning. As you continue your AI journey, you'll
learn how to build more advanced agents using machine learning and
natural language processing. But for now, take a moment to
celebrate your achievement. You've taken the first step toward
becoming an AI creator!

Chapter 7: Making Your Agent Smarter (Using LLMs)

Introduction: Setting the Stage

In the previous chapter, we built a rule-based chatbot that follows predefined "if-then" rules. While this is a great starting point, it's time to take our AI agent to the next level by integrating **Large Language Models (LLMs)**. LLMs are the brains behind advanced AI applications like ChatGPT, and they'll allow our agent to understand and generate human-like language.

Imagine our chatbot evolving from simply following pre-defined rules to actually understanding the meaning behind your words and generating thoughtful, context-aware responses. That's the power of LLMs! In this chapter, we'll use free APIs, like the **OpenAI API**, to connect our agent to these powerful language models.

We'll learn how to use **prompts** effectively to get our agent to answer questions, generate ideas, and hold conversations. We'll also explore how to add **memory** to our agent, allowing it to remember past conversations and provide more personalized responses.

By the end of this chapter, you'll have a conversational AI agent that can understand and respond to user input in a much more natural and engaging way. Let's get started!

Connecting Your AI Agent to an LLM

To make our chatbot smarter, we'll connect it to an LLM using the **OpenAI API**. Here's how to do it step by step.

Step 1: Install the OpenAI Library

1. Open your Google Colab notebook.

2. In a new code cell, type the following command and run it:

python
Copy

```
!pip install openai
```

Step 2: Import the OpenAI Library

In a new code cell, type the following code and run it:

python
Copy

```
import openai
import os
```

Step 3: Set Your OpenAI API Key

1. You'll need an **OpenAI API key** to access the LLM. If you don't have one, create an account on the OpenAI website and generate an API key.

2. In a new code cell, type the following code and replace `"YOUR_API_KEY"` with your actual API key:

python
Copy

```
os.environ["OPENAI_API_KEY"] = "YOUR_API_KEY"
openai.api_key = os.getenv("OPENAI_API_KEY")
```

Step 4: Create a Function to Interact with the LLM

In a new code cell, type the following code and run it:

python
Copy

```
def get_llm_response(prompt):
    response = openai.Completion.create(
        engine="text-davinci-003",   # Or another
suitable engine
        prompt=prompt,
        max_tokens=150,   # Adjust as needed
        temperature=0.7,   # Adjust for creativity
```

```
    )
    return response.choices[0].text.strip()
```

Step 5: Integrate the LLM into Your Chatbot

Modify your chatbot code to use the `get_llm_response()` function:

python
Copy

```python
def chatbot():
    print("Hello! I'm your smarter chatbot.")

    while True:
        user_input = input("You: ")

        if user_input.lower() == "bye" or
user_input.lower() == "goodbye":
            print("Chatbot: Goodbye!")
            break
        else:
            prompt = f"User: {user_input}\nChatbot:"
            response = get_llm_response(prompt)
            print(f"Chatbot: {response}")

chatbot()
```

Explanation of the Code

- `!pip install openai`: Installs the OpenAI library.

- `import openai`: Imports the OpenAI library.

- `os.environ["OPENAI_API_KEY"]`: Sets your OpenAI API key as an environment variable.

- `get_llm_response(prompt)`: Sends a prompt to the OpenAI API and returns the LLM's response.

- `chatbot()`: Integrates the LLM into your chatbot, allowing it to generate human-like responses.

Using Prompts Effectively

Now that our chatbot is connected to an LLM, let's learn how to craft effective prompts to get the desired output.

1. Be Clear and Specific

The more specific your prompt, the better the LLM will understand your request. For example:

python
Copy

```
prompt = "Write a short poem about nature."
response = get_llm_response(prompt)
print(response)
```

2. Provide Context

Give the LLM enough context to understand your request. For example:

python
Copy

```
article = "..."   # Insert your article here
prompt = f"Summarize the main points of this article:
{article}"
response = get_llm_response(prompt)
print(response)
```

3. Use Examples

If you want the LLM to generate a specific type of output, provide examples. For example:

python
Copy

```
prompt = "Write a story in the style of Edgar Allan
Poe."
response = get_llm_response(prompt)
print(response)
```

4. Experiment and Refine

Don't be afraid to experiment with different prompts and refine them until you get the desired output. For example:

python
Copy

```python
prompt = "What is the capital of France?"
response = get_llm_response(prompt)
print(response)
```

Building a Conversational AI Agent

Let's make our agent more conversational by adding **memory** and **context**.

1. Store Conversation History

We can store the conversation history in a list to provide context for the LLM:

python
Copy

```python
conversation_history = []

def chatbot():
    print("Hello! I'm your conversational chatbot.")

    while True:
        user_input = input("You: ")

        if user_input.lower() == "bye" or
user_input.lower() == "goodbye":
            print("Chatbot: Goodbye!")
            break
        else:
            conversation_history.append(f"User:
{user_input}")
            prompt = "\n".join(conversation_history) +
"\nChatbot:"
            response = get_llm_response(prompt)
```

```
            print(f"Chatbot: {response}")
            conversation_history.append(f"Chatbot:
{response}")

chatbot()
```

2. Limit Conversation History

To prevent the conversation history from becoming too long, we can
limit it:

python
Copy

```
conversation_history = []
max_history = 5  # Number of turns to remember.

def chatbot():
    print("Hello! I'm your conversational chatbot.")

    while True:
        user_input = input("You: ")

        if user_input.lower() == "bye" or
user_input.lower() == "goodbye":
            print("Chatbot: Goodbye!")
            break
        else:
            conversation_history.append(f"User:
{user_input}")
            prompt = "\n".join(conversation_history) +
"\nChatbot:"
            response = get_llm_response(prompt)
            print(f"Chatbot: {response}")
            conversation_history.append(f"Chatbot:
{response}")

            if len(conversation_history) > max_history
* 2:   # User and AI responses.
                conversation_history =
conversation_history[-max_history * 2:]

chatbot()
```

3. Add "Memory" to Your Agent

By storing the conversation history, our agent can remember past interactions and provide more context-aware responses. For example:

python
Copy

```python
conversation_history = []

def chatbot():
    print("Hello! I'm your conversational chatbot.")

    while True:
        user_input = input("You: ")

        if user_input.lower() == "bye" or
user_input.lower() == "goodbye":
            print("Chatbot: Goodbye!")
            break
        else:
            conversation_history.append(f"User:
{user_input}")
            prompt = "\n".join(conversation_history) +
"\nChatbot:"
            response = get_llm_response(prompt)
            print(f"Chatbot: {response}")
            conversation_history.append(f"Chatbot:
{response}")

chatbot()
```

Conclusion: Your Smarter AI Agent is Ready!

Congratulations! You've transformed your rule-based chatbot into a smarter, more conversational AI agent by integrating an LLM. By using effective prompts and adding memory, your agent can now understand and respond to user input in a much more natural and engaging way.

This is just the beginning. As you continue your AI journey, you'll discover even more ways to enhance your agent's capabilities. For now, take a moment to celebrate your achievement—you've built an intelligent conversational AI agent!

Chapter 8: Building Autonomous AI Agents (AutoGPT/BabyAGI)

Introduction: Setting the Stage

In the previous chapters, we've explored how to build rule-based chatbots and agents powered by Large Language Models (LLMs). Now, it's time to take a giant leap forward and venture into the exciting realm of **autonomous AI agents**. These agents can set their own goals, plan their actions, and execute them without constant human intervention. Imagine an AI that can research topics, write code, manage projects, and even solve complex problems—all on its own!

This chapter will introduce you to two powerful frameworks for building autonomous AI agents: **AutoGPT** and **BabyAGI**. These tools leverage the power of LLMs to create agents that can think and act independently. We'll guide you through the process of setting up and running these frameworks, setting goals for your agents, and expanding their capabilities using plugins and APIs.

By the end of this chapter, you'll have a working autonomous AI agent that can tackle a wide range of tasks. Let's dive in and start building!

What Are Autonomous AI Agents?

Autonomous AI agents are a type of AI that can operate independently, without constant human oversight. They can perceive their environment, set goals, plan actions, and execute those actions to achieve their objectives. Here's a breakdown of their key characteristics:

1. Goal-Oriented

Autonomous agents can set and pursue goals. For example, you can ask an agent to "research the history of AI" or "write a blog post about autonomous AI agents."

2. Planning

They can create plans to achieve their goals. This involves breaking down complex tasks into smaller, manageable steps.

3. Action Execution

They can execute actions to carry out their plans. This might include searching the internet, writing code, or interacting with APIs.

4. Learning

They can learn from their experiences and adapt their behavior. For example, an agent might refine its search strategies based on past results.

5. Interaction

They can interact with their environment and other agents. This includes communicating with users, accessing external data, and collaborating with other AI systems.

Examples of Autonomous AI Agents

- **Research and Information Gathering**: Agents can search the internet, analyze data, and summarize information.

- **Task Automation**: Agents can automate complex tasks, such as writing code, managing projects, or creating content.

- **Problem Solving**: Agents can solve problems by breaking them down into smaller steps and finding solutions.

Autonomous AI agents are made possible by advancements in **Large Language Models (LLMs)**, which provide the reasoning and planning capabilities essential for building these agents.

Using AutoGPT and BabyAGI

Let's get started by setting up and running **AutoGPT** and **BabyAGI**. These frameworks will serve as the foundation for building your autonomous AI agents.

Step 1: Install AutoGPT or BabyAGI

1. Open your Google Colab notebook.

2. In a new code cell, type the following command to clone the respective repository:

   - For **AutoGPT**:

python
Copy

```
!git clone https://github.com/Significant-
Gravitas/Auto-GPT.git
```

   - For **BabyAGI**:

python
Copy

```
!git clone https://github.com/yoheinakajima/babyagi.git
```

3. Change the directory to the cloned repository:

   - For **AutoGPT**:

python
Copy

```
%cd Auto-GPT
```

- For **BabyAGI**:

python
Copy

```
%cd babyagi
```

4. Install the required dependencies:

python
Copy

```
!pip install -r requirements.txt
```

Step 2: Set Up Environment Variables

1. You'll need to set your **OpenAI API key** as an environment variable.

2. In a new code cell, type the following code and replace `"YOUR_API_KEY"` with your actual API key:

python
Copy

```
import os
os.environ["OPENAI_API_KEY"] = "YOUR_API_KEY"
```

Step 3: Run AutoGPT or BabyAGI

1. For **AutoGPT**:

- Rename the `env.template` file to `.env` and fill in your API keys.

- Run the following command:

python
Copy

```
!python scripts/main.py
```

2. For **BabyAGI**:

- Run the following command:

python
Copy

```
!python babyagi.py
```

Step 4: Set Goals for Your AI Agent

When you run AutoGPT or BabyAGI, you'll be prompted to enter goals for your agent. Be clear and specific about your goals. For example:

- "Research the history of AI."

- "Write a blog post about autonomous AI agents."

- "Find the best free online AI courses."

Step 5: Monitor Your AI Agent

AutoGPT and BabyAGI will generate output as they work towards their goals. Pay attention to the agent's actions and provide feedback if necessary.

Using Plugins and APIs

To make your autonomous AI agents even more powerful, you can extend their capabilities using **plugins** and **APIs**.

1. Plugins

Plugins are extensions that add new functionality to AutoGPT. You can find plugins on the AutoGPT GitHub repository or create your own. Follow the instructions in the plugin's documentation to install and use it.

2. APIs

APIs allow AutoGPT and BabyAGI to access external services and data. For example, you can use APIs to access weather data, stock prices, or social media feeds. Here's how to integrate an API into your agent:

Example: Using a Search API

Let's use a search API to allow your agent to search the internet:

python
Copy

```python
import requests

def search_internet(query):
    # Replace with your search API endpoint and key
    url = f"https://api.example.com/search?q={query}&key=YOUR_API_KEY"
    response = requests.get(url)
    if response.status_code == 200:
        return response.json()
    else:
        return None

# Integrate into AutoGPT/BabyAGI
results = search_internet("autonomous AI agents")
if results:
    # Process and use the search results
    print(results)
```

Conclusion: Your Autonomous AI Agent is Ready!

Congratulations! You've built an autonomous AI agent using AutoGPT or BabyAGI. By setting goals, integrating plugins, and leveraging APIs, you've created an agent that can think and act independently. This is just the beginning—autonomous AI agents have the potential to revolutionize how we work, learn, and solve problems.

As you continue your AI journey, experiment with different goals, plugins, and APIs to expand your agent's capabilities. The possibilities are endless, and you're now equipped to explore them. Happy building!

Chapter 9: Fun AI Agent Projects for Students

Introduction: Setting the Stage

We've covered the basics of building AI agents, from rule-based chatbots to conversational agents powered by LLMs. Now, it's time to put your skills to the test with some **fun and practical projects**! This chapter is all about getting creative and building AI agents that are not only educational but also entertaining.

We'll focus on projects that are relevant to students' lives, such as **study buddies**, **homework helpers**, **creative story generators**, and **task management assistants**. These projects will allow you to apply the concepts you've learned and explore the exciting possibilities of AI.

Each project comes with clear instructions, code examples, and tips for customization. We'll also encourage you to experiment and add your own personal touch. Remember, the goal is to **have fun and learn by doing**!

By the end of this chapter, you'll have a portfolio of AI agent projects that you can share with your friends and teachers. Let's get started!

Project 1: Study Buddy AI Agent

Let's build a **Study Buddy AI Agent** that can help you with flashcards, quizzes, and study schedules.

Project Description

This AI agent will help you study by:

- Creating and managing **flashcards**.

- Generating **quizzes** based on your study material.

- Organizing your **study schedule**.

Instructions

1. Create Flashcards

Flashcards are a great way to memorize information. Let's create a simple flashcard system using Python.

python
Copy

```python
# Step 1: Create a list of flashcards (questions and answers)
flashcards = [
    {"question": "What is the capital of France?", "answer": "Paris"},
    {"question": "What is 2 + 2?", "answer": "4"},
    {"question": "What is the chemical symbol for water?", "answer": "H2O"},
]

# Step 2: Create a function to randomly select a flashcard
import random

def ask_flashcard():
    card = random.choice(flashcards)
    print(f"Question: {card['question']}")
    user_answer = input("Your answer: ")
    if user_answer.lower() == card["answer"].lower():
        print("Correct! 🎉")
    else:
        print(f"Wrong! The correct answer is: {card['answer']}")

# Step 3: Test the flashcard system
ask_flashcard()
```

2. Generate Quizzes

Let's expand the flashcard system to generate quizzes.

python

Copy

```python
def generate_quiz(num_questions=3):
    score = 0
    for i in range(num_questions):
        print(f"\nQuestion {i + 1}:")
        ask_flashcard()
        score += 1
    print(f"\nQuiz complete! Your score:
{score}/{num_questions}")

# Step 4: Test the quiz system
generate_quiz()
```

3. Organize Study Schedules

Let's create a simple study schedule organizer.

python

Copy

```python
# Step 5: Create a study schedule
study_schedule = {
    "Monday": "Math - Chapter 1",
    "Tuesday": "Science - Chapter 2",
    "Wednesday": "History - Chapter 3",
    "Thursday": "English - Chapter 4",
    "Friday": "Review all chapters",
}

# Step 6: Create a function to display the schedule
def show_schedule():
    print("\nYour Study Schedule:")
    for day, task in study_schedule.items():
        print(f"{day}: {task}")

# Step 7: Test the schedule system
show_schedule()
```

4. Combine Everything into a Study Buddy

Now, let's combine the flashcard, quiz, and schedule systems into a single **Study Buddy AI Agent**.

python
Copy

```python
def study_buddy():
    print("Welcome to your Study Buddy AI Agent!")
    while True:
        print("\nWhat would you like to do?")
        print("1. Practice Flashcards")
        print("2. Take a Quiz")
        print("3. View Study Schedule")
        print("4. Exit")
        choice = input("Enter your choice (1-4): ")

        if choice == "1":
            ask_flashcard()
        elif choice == "2":
            generate_quiz()
        elif choice == "3":
            show_schedule()
        elif choice == "4":
            print("Goodbye! Happy studying! 📚")
            break
        else:
            print("Invalid choice. Please try again.")

# Step 8: Run the Study Buddy AI Agent
study_buddy()
```

Project 2: Homework Helper AI Agent

Let's build a **Homework Helper AI Agent** that can assist with solving math problems, explaining concepts, and providing study resources.

Project Description

This AI agent will:

- Solve basic math problems.

- Explain concepts in simple terms.

- Provide links to study resources.

Instructions

1. Solve Math Problems

Let's create a function to solve basic math problems.

python
Copy

```python
def solve_math_problem():
    problem = input("Enter a math problem (e.g., 2 +
2): ")
    try:
        result = eval(problem)
        print(f"The answer is: {result}")
    except:
        print("Sorry, I couldn't solve that problem.")

# Step 1: Test the math solver
solve_math_problem()
```

2. Explain Concepts

Let's create a function to explain concepts using an LLM.

python
Copy

```python
import openai

def explain_concept(concept):
    response = openai.Completion.create(
        engine="text-davinci-003",
        prompt=f"Explain {concept} in simple terms.",
        max_tokens=100,
    )
    print(response.choices[0].text.strip())

# Step 2: Test the concept explainer
explain_concept("photosynthesis")
```

3. Provide Study Resources

Let's create a function to provide links to study resources.

python
Copy

```python
def provide_resources(topic):
    resources = {
        "math": "https://www.khanacademy.org/math",
        "science":
"https://www.khanacademy.org/science",
        "history": "https://www.history.com",
        "english": "https://www.grammarly.com/blog",
    }
    if topic in resources:
        print(f"Here are some resources for {topic}:
{resources[topic]}")
    else:
        print(f"Sorry, I don't have resources for
{topic}.")

# Step 3: Test the resource provider
provide_resources("math")
```

4. Combine Everything into a Homework Helper

Now, let's combine the math solver, concept explainer, and resource provider into a single **Homework Helper AI Agent**.

python
Copy

```python
def homework_helper():
    print("Welcome to your Homework Helper AI Agent!")
    while True:
        print("\nWhat do you need help with?")
        print("1. Solve a Math Problem")
        print("2. Explain a Concept")
        print("3. Get Study Resources")
        print("4. Exit")
        choice = input("Enter your choice (1-4): ")

        if choice == "1":
            solve_math_problem()
        elif choice == "2":
```

```
            concept = input("Enter the concept you want
explained: ")
            explain_concept(concept)
        elif choice == "3":
            topic = input("Enter the topic you need
resources for: ")
            provide_resources(topic)
        elif choice == "4":
            print("Goodbye! Happy studying! 📚")
            break
        else:
            print("Invalid choice. Please try again.")

# Step 4: Run the Homework Helper AI Agent
homework_helper()
```

Project 3: Creative Story Generator AI Agent

Let's build a **Creative Story Generator AI Agent** that can generate fun and imaginative stories.

Project Description

This AI agent will:

- Generate stories based on user input (e.g., characters, setting, plot).

- Allow users to customize the story length and style.

Instructions

1. Generate Stories

Let's create a function to generate stories using an LLM.

python
Copy

```
def generate_story(character, setting, plot):
    prompt = f"Write a short story about {character} in
{setting} where {plot}."
    response = openai.Completion.create(
        engine="text-davinci-003",
```

```
        prompt=prompt,
        max_tokens=200,
    )
    print(response.choices[0].text.strip())

# Step 1: Test the story generator
generate_story("a brave knight", "a magical forest",
"they must rescue a lost treasure")
```

2. Customize Story Length and Style

Let's add options to customize the story length and style.

python
Copy

```
def generate_custom_story(character, setting, plot,
length="short", style="funny"):
    prompt = f"Write a {length} {style} story about
{character} in {setting} where {plot}."
    response = openai.Completion.create(
        engine="text-davinci-003",
        prompt=prompt,
        max_tokens=200,
    )
    print(response.choices[0].text.strip())

# Step 2: Test the custom story generator
generate_custom_story("a mischievous cat", "a small
town", "they cause chaos", length="long",
style="adventurous")
```

3. Combine Everything into a Story Generator

Now, let's combine the story generator into a single **Creative Story Generator AI Agent**.

python
Copy

```
def story_generator():
    print("Welcome to your Creative Story Generator AI
Agent!")
    while True:
        print("\nWhat kind of story would you like to
create?")
```

```
        character = input("Enter a character: ")
        setting = input("Enter a setting: ")
        plot = input("Enter a plot: ")
        length = input("Enter story length
(short/long): ")
        style = input("Enter story style
(funny/adventurous/mysterious): ")
        generate_custom_story(character, setting, plot,
length, style)
        choice = input("\nGenerate another story?
(yes/no): ")
        if choice.lower() != "yes":
            print("Goodbye! Happy storytelling! 📖")
            break

# Step 3: Run the Story Generator AI Agent
story_generator()
```

Conclusion: Your AI Agent Portfolio is Ready!

Congratulations! You've built three fun and practical AI agent projects: a **Study Buddy**, a **Homework Helper**, and a **Creative Story Generator**. These projects showcase the power of AI and how it can be applied to solve real-world problems and spark creativity.

Feel free to customize these projects further and share them with your friends and teachers. The possibilities are endless, and you're now equipped to explore them. Happy coding!

Chapter 10: Troubleshooting and Tips for Success

Introduction: Setting the Stage

Building AI agents is an exciting and rewarding process, but just like any journey, it comes with its share of challenges. You might encounter unexpected errors, your code might not behave as you expect, or you might simply feel stuck. That's perfectly normal! This chapter is your toolkit for navigating those hurdles, ensuring your AI agent projects are successful and your learning experience is smooth.

We'll start by diving into **common coding mistakes**, providing clear examples and practical solutions to help you fix errors and debug your code effectively. Then, we'll walk you through a **step-by-step troubleshooting guide**, giving you a structured approach to identifying and resolving issues.

Beyond debugging, we'll explore the vast resources available to you, including **online forums, communities, and documentation**. We'll also share tips for **continuous learning**, recommending free courses, books, and tools that will empower you to grow your AI agent skills.

This chapter is designed to build your confidence and equip you with the knowledge and resources you need to overcome any obstacle. By the end of this chapter, you'll be a more resilient and resourceful AI agent developer.

Common Coding Mistakes: How to Fix Errors and Debug Your Code

Let's tackle the common coding mistakes that beginners often encounter. Understanding these errors and how to fix them will significantly boost your debugging skills.

1. Syntax Errors

- **What they are**: These errors occur when you violate the rules of Python's grammar. Missing colons, incorrect indentation, or mismatched parentheses are common culprits.

- **Example**:

python
Copy

```
if x > 5
```

```
print("x is greater than 5")
```

Error Message: `SyntaxError: expected ':'`

- **How to fix**: Carefully review the line indicated by the error message. Ensure proper syntax, including colons, indentation, and matching parentheses/brackets.

- **Debugging Tip**: Pay close attention to the line numbers in error messages.

---

2. Name Errors

- **What they are**: These errors occur when you try to use a variable or function that hasn't been defined yet.

- **Example**:

python
Copy

```
print(user_name)
```

Error Message: `NameError: name 'user_name' is not defined`

- **How to fix**: Define the variable or function before using it. Double-check the spelling of your variable and function names.

- **Debugging Tip**: Use a code editor that highlights undefined variables.

---

3. Type Errors

- **What they are**: These errors occur when you try to perform an operation on incompatible data types.

- **Example**:

python
Copy

```
age = "25"
print(age + 10)
```

Error Message: `TypeError: can only concatenate str (not "int") to str`

- **How to fix**: Use the correct data types for your operations. Convert data types using functions like `int()`, `str()`, or `float()` when necessary.

- **Debugging Tip**: Use the `type()` function to check the data type of variables.

---

4. Index Errors

- **What they are**: These errors occur when you try to access an element in a list or string that doesn't exist.

- **Example**:

python
Copy

```
my_list = [1, 2, 3]
print(my_list[3])
```

Error Message: `IndexError: list index out of range`

- **How to fix**: Ensure your index is within the valid range of the list or string. Use the `len()` function to check the length of your data structures.

- **Debugging Tip**: Remember that list indices start at 0.

5. Logic Errors

- **What they are**: These errors occur when your code runs without crashing, but it doesn't produce the expected output due to flaws in your logic.

- **Example**:

python
Copy

```python
def is_positive(x):
    if x < 0:
        return True   # Incorrect logic
    else:
        return False
```

- **How to fix**: Carefully review your code's logic and use `print` statements to trace the execution flow and variable values. Break down complex logic into smaller, testable parts.

- **Debugging Tip**: Use a debugger to step through your code line by line.

Tips for Debugging: Step-by-Step Troubleshooting Guide

When you encounter an error, follow this systematic approach:

1. Read the Error Message Carefully

- Don't panic! Error messages are your friends. They provide valuable clues about the problem.

- Pay attention to the error type and the line number where the error occurred.

2. Isolate the Problem

- Try to reproduce the error in a simplified version of your code.

- Comment out sections of your code to narrow down the source of the error.

3. Use Print Statements

- Insert `print()` statements at strategic points in your code to check the values of variables and the execution flow.

- This can help you identify where the code is deviating from your expectations.

4. Use a Debugger (pdb)

- Python's `pdb` module allows you to step through your code line by line, inspect variables, and set breakpoints.

- Import `pdb` and insert `pdb.set_trace()` at the point where you want to start debugging.

- Learn the debugger commands (`n` for next, `s` for step, `c` for continue, `p` for print).

5. Search Online

- Copy and paste the error message into a search engine.

- **Stack Overflow** and other forums are excellent resources for finding solutions to common coding problems.

6. Ask for Help

- If you're still stuck, don't hesitate to ask for help from your classmates, teachers, or online communities.

- Provide clear and concise information about the problem, including the error message and relevant code snippets.

Where to Find Help: Online Forums, Communities, and Resources

Here are some essential resources for finding help and support:

1. Online Forums

- **Stack Overflow**: A massive Q&A site for programmers.
- **Reddit**: Subreddits like `r/learnpython`, `r/python`, and `r/MachineLearning`.

2. Communities

- **GitHub**: Explore open-source projects, contribute to the community, and find code examples.
- **Discord Servers**: Join communities related to Python or AI.

3. Documentation

- **Official Python Documentation**: A comprehensive resource for Python language information.
- **Library Documentation**: Most Python libraries have detailed documentation.

How to Keep Learning: Recommendations for Free Courses, Books, and Tools

Continue your learning journey with these resources:

1. Free Courses

- **Coursera's "Python for Everybody" Specialization**.
- **edX's "Introduction to Python Programming"**.
- **FreeCodeCamp's Python Curriculum**.

2. Books

- **"Automate the Boring Stuff with Python"** by Al Sweigart.

- **"Python Crash Course"** by Eric Matthes.

- **"Hands-On Machine Learning with Scikit-Learn, Keras, and TensorFlow"** by Aurélien Géron.

3. Tools

- **VS Code** or **PyCharm** (code editors).

- **Google Colab** (online Python environment).

- **Jupyter Notebooks** (interactive computing).

- **Git** (version control).

Conclusion: You're Ready to Succeed!

By understanding common coding mistakes, mastering debugging techniques, and leveraging the wealth of resources available, you're well-equipped to overcome any challenge that comes your way. Remember, every problem is an opportunity to learn and grow. Keep practicing, stay curious, and most importantly, have fun on your AI agent journey!

Part 3: The Future of AI Agents (And Your Role)

Chapter 11: AI Agents in the Real World

Introduction: Setting the Stage

We've explored the theoretical foundations and practical development of AI agents, building them from the ground up. Now, it's time to step out of the lab and see how these agents are making a tangible difference in the real world. This chapter will showcase the diverse applications of AI agents across various industries, demonstrating their transformative power.

We'll delve into how AI agents are revolutionizing **healthcare**, reshaping **education**, and enhancing **entertainment** experiences. We'll also examine the broader impact of AI agents on society, exploring how they're changing the way we live and work.

To bring these concepts to life, we'll explore **real-world case studies**, showcasing how AI agents are being used to solve complex problems and create innovative solutions. By the end of this chapter, you'll have a clear understanding of the practical applications of AI agents and their profound impact on our world.

AI Agents in Different Industries

AI agents are no longer confined to research labs; they're actively deployed across a wide range of industries, driving innovation and efficiency. Let's explore some of these applications.

1. Healthcare

AI agents are transforming healthcare by improving diagnosis, treatment, and patient care.

- **Diagnosis and Treatment**: AI agents analyze medical images, patient data, and research papers to assist doctors in diagnosing diseases and developing personalized treatment plans.

- **Virtual Assistants**: Chatbots provide patient support, answer medical queries, and schedule appointments.

- **Drug Discovery**: AI agents accelerate drug discovery by analyzing vast datasets and predicting the efficacy of potential drug candidates.

Example: IBM Watson

IBM Watson is used to analyze medical records and research papers, assisting doctors in diagnosing cancer and developing personalized treatment plans. Watson has been shown to improve diagnostic accuracy and accelerate drug discovery.

---

2. Education

AI agents are reshaping education by personalizing learning and automating administrative tasks.

- **Personalized Learning**: AI agents adapt to individual learning styles, providing customized content and feedback.

- **Virtual Tutors**: AI-powered tutors offer personalized instruction and support, helping students master complex concepts.

- **Automated Grading**: AI agents automate the grading of assignments, freeing up teachers' time for more personalized instruction.

Example: Duolingo

Duolingo uses AI agents to personalize language learning experiences, adapting to individual learning styles and providing customized feedback. AI algorithms analyze user progress and adjust the difficulty of lessons.

---

3. Entertainment

AI agents are enhancing entertainment experiences by creating personalized content and improving recommendations.

- **Content Creation**: AI agents generate personalized content, such as music, art, and stories.

- **Gaming**: AI agents create realistic and challenging game environments, enhancing the gaming experience.

- **Recommendation Systems**: AI agents analyze user preferences to recommend movies, music, and other content.

Example: Netflix

Netflix uses AI agents to analyze user preferences and viewing history, recommending movies and TV shows that users are likely to enjoy. This personalized recommendation system enhances user engagement and satisfaction.

---

4. Finance

AI agents are optimizing financial services by improving fraud detection, trading, and customer service.

- **Fraud Detection**: AI agents detect fraudulent transactions and suspicious activities.

- **Algorithmic Trading**: AI agents automate trading decisions, optimizing investment strategies.

- **Customer Service**: Chatbots provide instant customer support and answer financial queries.

Example: JP Morgan's COIN

JP Morgan uses AI to analyze legal documents, reducing the time spent on manual review. COIN has significantly improved efficiency in contract review.

---

5. Manufacturing

AI agents are revolutionizing manufacturing by automating processes and improving quality control.

- **Robotics**: AI-powered robots automate manufacturing processes, improving efficiency and productivity.

- **Quality Control**: AI agents inspect products for defects, ensuring quality and consistency.

- **Predictive Maintenance**: AI agents predict equipment failures, allowing for proactive maintenance and minimizing downtime.

---

6. Transportation

AI agents are transforming transportation by enabling autonomous vehicles and optimizing logistics.

- **Autonomous Vehicles**: AI agents enable self-driving cars and trucks, improving safety and efficiency.

- **Traffic Management**: AI agents optimize traffic flow, reducing congestion and travel times.

- **Logistics**: AI agents optimize delivery routes and manage supply chains.

Example: Waymo

Waymo's self-driving cars use AI agents to perceive their environment, make driving decisions, and navigate roads safely. Waymo has logged millions of miles in autonomous driving, demonstrating the potential of AI in transportation.

The Impact of AI Agents on Society

AI agents are transforming the way we live and work, bringing both opportunities and challenges.

1. Increased Efficiency and Productivity

- AI agents automate repetitive tasks, freeing up human workers to focus on more creative and strategic work.

- They optimize processes and improve decision-making, leading to increased efficiency and productivity.

2. Enhanced Decision-Making

- AI agents analyze vast amounts of data, providing insights that humans might miss.

- They help us make more informed decisions in various fields, from healthcare to finance.

3. Improved Accessibility

- AI agents provide assistive technologies for people with disabilities, enhancing their independence and quality of life.

- They also provide access to information and services for people in remote areas.

4. Job Displacement

- Automation may lead to job losses in certain sectors, requiring workforce retraining and adaptation.

5. Ethical Concerns

- **AI Bias**: AI systems can perpetuate biases present in their training data.

- **Privacy and Security**: The use of AI raises concerns about data privacy and security.

- **Autonomous Weapons**: The use of AI in autonomous weapons raises profound ethical questions.

6. Social Impact

- AI agents are changing social interactions, communication, and information consumption.

- It is vital to ensure that AI is used to promote social good and equity.

Real-World Examples: Case Studies of AI Agents in Action

Let's explore some real-world examples of AI agents making a difference.

1. IBM Watson in Healthcare

IBM Watson is used to analyze medical records and research papers, assisting doctors in diagnosing cancer and developing personalized treatment plans. Watson has been shown to improve diagnostic accuracy and accelerate drug discovery.

2. Duolingo's AI-Powered Language Learning

Duolingo uses AI agents to personalize language learning experiences, adapting to individual learning styles and providing customized feedback. AI algorithms analyze user progress and adjust the difficulty of lessons.

3. Netflix's Recommendation System

Netflix uses AI agents to analyze user preferences and viewing history, recommending movies and TV shows that users are likely to enjoy. This personalized recommendation system enhances user engagement and satisfaction.

4. Waymo's Self-Driving Cars

Waymo's self-driving cars use AI agents to perceive their environment, make driving decisions, and navigate roads safely.

Waymo has logged millions of miles in autonomous driving, demonstrating the potential of AI in transportation.

5. JP Morgan's COIN (Contract Intelligence)

JP Morgan uses AI to analyze legal documents, reducing the time spent on manual review. COIN has significantly improved efficiency in contract review.

Conclusion: AI Agents Are Transforming Our World

AI agents are no longer just a futuristic concept—they're here, and they're making a real impact across industries and society. From healthcare and education to entertainment and transportation, AI agents are driving innovation, improving efficiency, and enhancing our quality of life.

However, as we embrace these advancements, it's crucial to address the ethical and societal challenges they bring. By doing so, we can ensure that AI agents are used responsibly and equitably, benefiting everyone.

As you continue your journey in AI, remember that the possibilities are endless. Whether you're building AI agents to solve complex problems or creating innovative solutions, you're contributing to a future where AI transforms our world for the better.

Chapter 12: The Future of AI Agents and You

Introduction: Setting the Stage

We've journeyed through the world of AI agents, from building simple chatbots to exploring advanced concepts like reinforcement learning. Now, let's turn our gaze to the horizon and envision the future. The world you're stepping into is one where AI agents are not just tools, but **collaborators, problem-solvers, and even creative partners**.

This chapter isn't just about predicting the future; it's about empowering you to shape it. You're the generation that will define how AI impacts our lives. We'll explore the exciting possibilities that lie ahead, from **personalized education and healthcare** to **groundbreaking scientific discoveries** and **creative innovations**.

We'll also discuss the **ethical responsibilities** that come with this powerful technology, urging you to think critically about how AI agents can be used for good. This chapter is a **call to action**, inspiring you to become active participants in the AI revolution and to create a future where AI benefits everyone.

The Evolving Landscape of AI Agents

The pace of AI development is accelerating, and AI agents are becoming increasingly sophisticated. Here's a glimpse into the evolving landscape:

1. Hyper-Personalization

- Imagine AI agents that understand your individual needs and preferences on a deep level, providing truly personalized experiences in education, healthcare, and entertainment.

- AI agents will adapt to your learning style, anticipate your health needs, and curate content that resonates with your interests.

Example: Personalized Learning

AI tutors will tailor lessons to your strengths and weaknesses, ensuring you learn at your own pace and in a way that suits you best.

---

2. Autonomous Collaboration

- AI agents will be able to collaborate seamlessly with humans and other AI agents, forming dynamic teams to tackle complex problems.

- They'll handle routine tasks, allowing humans to focus on creative and strategic work.

Example: Scientific Research

AI agents will assist scientists by analyzing data, running simulations, and generating hypotheses, accelerating discoveries in fields like medicine and climate science.

---

3. Enhanced Creativity

- AI agents will become powerful creative tools, assisting artists, musicians, and writers in generating new ideas and pushing the boundaries of creativity.

- They'll be able to compose music, write stories, and create visual art in unique and innovative ways.

Example: AI-Generated Art

AI tools like DALL·E and MidJourney are already creating stunning visual art, and future AI agents will collaborate with artists to produce even more groundbreaking work.

---

4. Proactive Problem-Solving

- AI agents will be able to anticipate and prevent problems before they occur, from predicting equipment failures to identifying potential health risks.

- They'll analyze data in real-time to provide early warnings and actionable insights.

Example: Predictive Healthcare

AI agents will monitor your health data and alert you to potential issues before they become serious, enabling proactive and personalized care.

---

5. Ethical AI Agents

- As AI agents become more autonomous, ethical considerations will become paramount.

- Future AI agents will be designed with built-in ethical guidelines, ensuring fairness, transparency, and accountability.

Example: Bias Mitigation

AI systems will be trained to recognize and mitigate biases, ensuring fair outcomes in areas like hiring, lending, and law enforcement.

Your Role in Shaping the Future

You are not just a spectator in this AI revolution; you are a key player. Here's how you can prepare for and contribute to the future of AI agents:

1. Embrace Lifelong Learning

- The field of AI is constantly evolving, so continuous learning is essential.

- Stay curious, explore new technologies, and adapt to the changing landscape.

Actionable Tip: Take online courses, attend workshops, and read research papers to stay updated.

2. Develop Strong Ethical Foundations

- Understand the ethical implications of AI and develop a strong moral compass.

- Advocate for responsible AI development and use.

Actionable Tip: Study AI ethics and participate in discussions about the societal impact of AI.

3. Cultivate Interdisciplinary Skills

- AI is a multidisciplinary field, so develop skills in areas like programming, mathematics, data science, and ethics.

- Combine your technical skills with creative thinking and problem-solving abilities.

Actionable Tip: Explore fields like psychology, design, and sociology to understand how AI interacts with human behavior.

4. Become a Creator, Not Just a Consumer

- Don't just use AI tools; learn how to build them.

- Experiment with AI agent development and create innovative solutions.

Actionable Tip: Start small by building simple AI projects and gradually take on more complex challenges.

5. Collaborate and Communicate

- AI projects often involve collaboration with diverse teams.

- Develop strong communication and teamwork skills to work effectively with others.

Actionable Tip: Join AI communities, participate in hackathons, and collaborate on open-source projects.

6. Focus on Human-Centered AI

- Design AI agents that enhance human capabilities and improve the quality of life.

- Prioritize user experience and accessibility.

Actionable Tip: Conduct user research to understand the needs and challenges of the people who will use your AI solutions.

7. Be a Responsible Innovator

- Consider the potential impact of your AI projects on society and the environment.

- Strive to create AI solutions that are sustainable and equitable.

Actionable Tip: Evaluate the long-term consequences of your work and seek feedback from diverse stakeholders.

A Call to Action

The future of AI agents is not predetermined; it's being shaped by the choices we make today. You have the power to create a future where AI empowers us all.

- **Embrace your curiosity**: Challenge the status quo and dare to dream big.

- **Experiment and learn**: Don't be afraid to fail; every mistake is an opportunity to grow.

- **Collaborate and share**: Build a community of AI innovators and work together to solve global challenges.

- **Advocate for ethical AI**: Use your voice to ensure AI is developed and used responsibly.

- **Focus on impact**: Create AI solutions that address pressing issues like climate change, poverty, and healthcare.

The future of AI agents is in your hands. Let's work together to build a future where AI empowers us all to reach our full potential.

Conclusion: Embarking on the AI Agent Frontier

We've reached the culmination of our journey—a journey that has taken us from the foundational principles of AI agents to the cutting-edge frontiers of autonomous systems. We've explored the building blocks of intelligent agents, delved into the intricacies of language models, and grappled with the ethical considerations that shape the future of AI.

This book wasn't merely about imparting technical knowledge; it was about igniting a spark, fostering a sense of wonder, and empowering you to become active participants in the AI revolution. You've learned to construct rule-based chatbots, harness the power of Large Language Models, and even venture into the realm of autonomous agents. But more importantly, you've gained the confidence to experiment, to innovate, and to contribute to the ever-evolving landscape of artificial intelligence.

The Transformative Power of AI Agents

We've seen how AI agents are transforming industries, from healthcare and education to entertainment and finance. They're revolutionizing the way we diagnose diseases, personalize learning, create art, and manage finances. AI agents are not just tools; they're collaborators, problem-solvers, and creative partners. They have the potential to solve complex problems, enhance human capabilities, and create a more equitable and sustainable future.

Yet, with this power comes responsibility. Throughout this book, we've emphasized the importance of ethical considerations. As AI agents become more autonomous and influential, it's crucial to ensure they are designed with fairness, transparency, and accountability in mind. The future of AI must be shaped by human values, and you have a vital role to play in making that vision a reality.

Your Role in Shaping the Future

The future of AI agents is not a distant concept; it's being shaped by the actions we take today. As you step forward, remember that you are not just a consumer of technology; you are a creator, an innovator, and a steward of the future. The skills and knowledge you've gained in this book are your tools for building a better world.

1. Embrace Lifelong Learning

The field of AI is constantly evolving. New algorithms, tools, and applications are emerging every day. Stay curious, explore new technologies, and adapt to the changing landscape. Whether it's taking online courses, attending workshops, or reading research papers, never stop learning.

2. Experiment and Innovate

Don't be afraid to experiment, to fail, and to learn from your mistakes. Every challenge you overcome will make you a stronger and more resilient AI agent developer. Start small, build simple projects, and gradually take on more complex challenges. Innovation thrives on curiosity and persistence.

3. Collaborate and Share

AI is a collaborative field. Share your ideas, collaborate with others, and build a community of AI innovators. The collective intelligence of a community is far greater than the sum of its parts. Together, we can push the boundaries of AI and create solutions that benefit humanity.

4. Focus on Human-Centered AI

Design AI agents that enhance human capabilities, improve the quality of life, and promote inclusivity. Prioritize user experience and accessibility, ensuring that AI is accessible to everyone. Remember, the ultimate goal of AI is to serve humanity.

5. Be a Responsible Innovator

Consider the potential impact of your AI projects on society and the environment. Strive to create AI solutions that are sustainable, equitable, and aligned with human values. Advocate for ethical AI development and use, and ensure that your work contributes to the greater good.

The Journey Ahead

The journey of AI agent development is a marathon, not a sprint. There will be moments of frustration and moments of triumph. But with persistence, creativity, and a commitment to ethical principles, you can make a meaningful contribution to the AI revolution.

As you embark on your own AI agent adventures, remember that you are not alone. You are part of a global community of innovators, researchers, and enthusiasts who are passionate about shaping the future of AI. Embrace the challenge, seize the opportunity, and let your creativity soar.

A Final Word

The future of AI agents is in your hands. Whether you're building chatbots, designing autonomous systems, or exploring the ethical implications of AI, your work has the potential to make a lasting impact. The possibilities are endless, and the journey is just beginning.

So go forth, experiment, innovate, and create. Build AI agents that solve real-world problems, inspire creativity, and improve lives. Be a force for good in the AI revolution, and help shape a future where technology empowers us all to reach our full potential.

The frontier of AI agents awaits—embrace it with curiosity, courage, and a commitment to making the world a better place.

www.ingramcontent.com/pod-product-compliance
Lightning Source LLC
LaVergne TN
LVHW051715050326
832903LV00032B/4212